Transformation Meditation

Doubt Free Meditation

Foundation Series

Student Workbook

by Shree
Sherrie Wade, M.A.
Licensed Mental Health Counselor (#MH3015)
National Certified Counselor

The Doubt Free Mediation Foundation Series Course includes:

- *Infinite Peace Audio Recording* (CDs or mp3): Breathing techniques, guided meditations and progressive deep relaxation.

- *Certificate of Achievement* upon completion of 10-question multiple-choice quiz.

- *Email Support* from a Transformation Meditation Teacher for all registered students

Certificate of Achievement is awarded upon successful completion of the course and submission of the quiz and evaluation.

If you have completed this course and have not registered to receive your certificate you can register online at www.transformationmeditation.com

Published by
Transformation Meditation, Inc.
Boca Raton, Florida, USA

For more information, to contact the author,
or to order additional copies, please contact us at:

web: www.TransformationMeditation.com
e-mail: info@TransformationMeditation.com

Acknowledgements

To my beloved Guru Swami Shyam for his unprecedented and inspiring interpretations of the ancient texts as well as his tireless guidance and mentoring over the past fifteen years.

Many thanks to my husband, Alan Wade, for his constant love, support and advice, and to all the friends and family who helped me in this project.

The cover photo is of the lotus pond at India Habitat Center, New Delhi. The lotus flower symbolizes purity and spiritual perfection. It is firmly rooted in the mud but blossoms above the water, completely uncontaminated by the mud. To be seated on the lotus suggests that one has transcended the limitation of the finite world (the mud of existence) and floats freely in a sphere of purity and spirituality.

Cover photo:	Lindsay Smith
Cover design:	Sherrie Wade
Inside design:	Eric Myhr
Editing:	Alan Wade
Recording/music:	Alan Wade

TABLE OF CONTENTS

INTRODUCTION

Congratulations on registering for the Transformation Meditation, Doubt Free Meditation Foundation Series. This course has been taught successfully for over twenty years to people of all ages, walks of life, and cultures. It has proven to be one of the most highly effective methods of learning meditation. It is easy to understand and brings about immediate results!

Now, with this course, you can study the entire five-session series in the comfort of your own home or with a Transformation Meditation Instructor. You will receive a Certificate of Achievement when you successfully complete the 10-question multiple-choice quiz.

This course can be studied by focusing on one session at a time, maybe one per week depending on your time schedule. This will allow adequate practice time for the new techniques you are learning. The next page gives you suggestions of which material to study for each lesson.

Many techniques can be utilized in the practice of meditation. In this course we bring the attention, through several techniques, to the meditative state that underlies all the states of consciousness.

By following any thought to its source, you can experience that source or Knower that you are. And that Knower is pure, free and forever.

May you have much success in coming to know your true Self and enjoying the peace, serenity, and fulfillment that dwells within you!

How to Take This Course

Complete one session per week; reading and reflecting on the material for each session as listed below, following the instructions.

Five-Session Series: Lesson Plans

Session 1

1. What is Meditation - read and reflect (p. 7)

2. Mantra Meditation - read and practice (p. 9)

3. Meditate Now: Twelve Secrets to Easy and Perfect Meditation - read and reflect (p. 21)

4. The Sixteen Effects of Meditation - read and reflect (p. 25)

5. Guided meditation on *Infinite Peace* audio recording - follow the instructions given for the first 15-minute meditation on the *Infinite Peace* audio recording (CD or MP3)

Session 2

1. The Four States of Consciousness - read and reflect on this writing in your next meditation (p. 27)

2. Breathing Techniques - practice the deep, three-part breathing technique (first one given on the sheet) (p. 30-33)

3. This is Meditation – read and follow the instructions given for the second and third guided meditations given on the *Infinite Peace* audio recording (CD or MP3) (p. 34)

Session 3

1. How Stress Can Affect You - read and reflect (p. 29)

2. Breathing Techniques - practice the Alternate Nostril breathing technique (p. 32)

3. Transform the Stress Reaction Into Relaxation and Ease - read and practice (p. 36)

Session 4

1. Chart: Non-Meditator's Mind/Meditator's Mind (p. 38)

2. The De-identification Process - How to Stop Worrying and Enjoy Your Life; Six Steps to Freedom from Disturbing Thoughts and Feeling - go through this process step-by-step (p. 40)

3. Progressive Deep Relaxation - review the written sheet and then practice this technique using the *Infinite Peace* audio recording (CD or MP3) as a guide (p. 43)

Session 5

1. Breathing Techniques - practice the third meditation technique (track 3) on the *Infinite Peace* audio recording (CD or MP3)

2. Various Meditation Techniques - read and practice each of the techniques over the next week (p. 41)

3. Four Stages of Mantra Meditation - practice all the techniques on the audio recording while focusing your awareness on the four stages of mantra meditation (p. 45)

After the Sessions

Complete the 10-question multiple-choice quiz and course evalution form online using the links provided in your registration confirmation letter (you can e-mail us for the links at quiz@transformationmeditation.com). Upon successful completion of the course quiz and submitting your evaluation form online you will receive a certificate of acheivement.

Developing Your Home Practice

Now that you understand the nature of the meditative state you can practice anywhere at anytime!

To be sure to get the maximum benefit it is recommended that your practice at least 10-20 minutes in the morning and evening every day. You can use the Infinite Peace audio recording to help develop your meditation style and techniques. Eventually your meditation will become a part of you and you can practice on your own. Through this practice, and developing your understanding of the meditative state, you will begin to live the fourth state or consciousness (the meditative state) in your daily life.

It is also very helpful to read and study the books on our recommended reading list and the other courses and written materials that we offer on our website: www.transformationmeditation.com

This type of reading and listening to knowledge becomes an integral part of your *saadhanaa* (practice) and will greatly assist you in sitting silently for meditation.

What is Meditation?

M editation is the process of experiencing a state of pure awareness. Through calming the mind and emotions you can experience a state of peace and tranquility. Meditation is a simple technique that can be learned in a few minutes. To master it requires continued practice, guidance and mature knowledge of the process.

According to the science of meditation, optimum existence is experienced when the most subtle aspect of your thought leads you to the experience of peace or harmony. Subtle forms of thought are called waves of perception. Through the practice of meditation you can train yourself to de-identify with the passing thoughts or waves of perception that lead the attention towards identifying with stressful situations. Instead, you focus on the pure awareness state, also called the Knower or experiencer of thoughts. When you no longer identify or become mixed in any particular thought or physical sensation, then the space behind the thought, which is always peaceful, is experienced. This is termed by psychologists as a peak experience, the transpersonal self, and by yogic practitioners as the fourth state of consciousness.

Through the practice of meditation and the observation of your thoughts, you develop the power to discriminate between those thoughts that are useful and those that are not. The mind is seen as an instrument that is used to perceive the world. You can develop the power to observe your mental functioning and maintain the awareness that you are the observer of your mind. You can then choose which thoughts to identify with and which ones to act on, de-identifying with irrational or destructive thoughts or beliefs. These negative thoughts or waves of perception can be allowed to pass without holding on to them, or they can be observed as if watching them on a screen. As you focus on the consciousness out of which these thoughts or waves are arising, you are led to experience the peace that is at the back of the thought.

Thoughts have certain qualities. Some thoughts produce more stress by leading the attention towards worries, doubts, fears and skepticism. Thoughts that are positive can be retained; those that are negative can be released. You do not need to stop the flow of these thoughts; they do not create any problem unless you, the Self, identifies with them. The natural function of the mind is to think, and no thought is destructive if there is no effect from it.

Meditation allows you to spend time aware of yourself as the Self, or the Knower of all the thoughts and phenomena. From this state you can experience both negative and positive emotions and maintain the knowledge of the peaceful Self. The Knower state is always peaceful as it is the Pure Consciousness or life itself. Suffering occurs only when the Knower, forgetting its true nature, identifies with the thought of the mind and feelings of the physical body.

Meditation is known to relax the physiology and reverse the damaging effects of stress. So many people are feeling uneasy, isolated and lonely. These feelings can create tension, weaken the immune system and cause disease. The immune system is strengthened and healing is accelerated by developing a positive attitude and visualization of health. Using the Transformation Meditation system of meditation, the mind is trained to continuously focus on the life force or Pure Consciousness, even before the thought arises. In this way, the problem of having a negative attitude or belief system is taken care of at its source. This can save a lot of time and the effort of sorting through and trying to change an infinite number of negative thoughts and beliefs. In fact, it takes care of the problem before it even arises by focusing the attention at the source of the thought, or the Pure Consciousness state.

Mantra Meditation

Mantra meditation is a practical technique that blends the calming effect of soothing sound vibrations with the empowering knowledge of their meaning.

In Sanskrit, the original language of *Yog*, '*man*' means 'mind' and '*tra*' means 'release'. So *man-tra* evolved as a practical technique for the meditator to use to quickly and easily release the mind from its association and identification with undesirable thoughts, desires and mental impressions.

Essentially, any sound and its related meaning can be used as mantra; even, for example, your own name. The name, Alan, means 'harmony' in Celtic. Yet, the ancient Yogis, while practicing and developing the science of meditation, discovered that certain special sound vibrations had a much more profound and positive effect on the meditator in comparison to more regular, mundane sounds and words.

Om, for example, is universally used as a meditation mantra and is known as a 'seed' mantra because it contains all the elements of a pure sound vibration. It is such a simple, yet resonant sound (rhymes with home) that it always produces easiness and peace in anyone who sincerely repeats it softly and gently inside, silently, or outside, as a sonorous humming sound.

This sweet and gentle sound, *Om*, has a profound and inspiring meaning. As a symbolic sound, it represents the primordial vibration, the 'genesis' wave of manifestation, that is the source and essential, vibrational 'building block' upon which all other sounds, forms, experiences and changing phenomena are based upon. When gently repeated in meditation, as both sound vibration for the senses and powerful meaning for the mind, *Om* always produces a state of peace, clarity and highest awareness in the consciousness of the meditator.

This brings us to another important aspect of mantra meditation – repetition. By repeating the mantra, gently and sweetly, inside or outside, again and again, a profound experience of pure consciousness is created in the head and the heart of the meditator. And while repeating sound and meaning over and over, the mind and intellect of the meditator become purified and pacified. This repetition of mantra, sound with meaning, purifies the human mind of uneasy thought patterns, expands the intellect into its higher nature as pure awareness and fills the ego, I, with a profound sense of fullness, completion and perfection!

So, in review, the sound and meaning of a pure vibration, repeated regularly in meditation with sincerity and undivided focus, produces wonderful results in the head and heart of the meditator. Mantra meditation becomes a powerful catalyst for your unfoldment of the realized state!

Of course, you can still meditate without using a mantra. Yet, research – both ancient and contemporary – has shown, again and again, that repeating a mantra accelerates results in meditation and greatly enhances the capacity of the meditator to experience higher and subtler states of consciousness! So mantra is a very useful and integral tool for you to apply in your daily practice.

This leads us, naturally, to the mantra that has been recommended as the most beneficial and effective in practicing Transformation Meditation. The greatest mantra – *Amaram Hum, Madhuram Hum!*

Our meditation teacher, Swami Shyam, evolved this wonderfully profound sound mantra through his years and years of dedicated and unbroken meditation practice (since the tender age of seven!). His own highest awareness, evolved through years of long and dedicated practice, unfolded this mantra – *Amaram Hum Madhuram Hum* – for the benefit of all humanity. This mantra can be shared and resonated the world over as an effective and practical 'key' sound vibration that, when repeated one-pointedly and with regularity, unfolds a deep sense of oneness, harmony and peace in the one repeating and, ultimately, unlocks the mental doors of perception to Self Realization!

The meditator becomes the mantra! There's no separation between the one repeating mantra, the mantra being repeated and the relationship between repeater and repeated. The meditator, through perfected practice of mantra meditation, comes to directly know mantra as his own self, his own being, one pure field of existence, undivided, all-permeating and without end or beginning!

So what does *Amaram Hum, Madhuram Hum* mean? And how do I repeat it properly, with the right pronunciation and correct awareness? Good and timely questions!

Amaram Hum, Madhuram Hum is an ancient Sanskrit phrase. '*Amar*' translates as undying, unborn, and, therefore, infinite, eternal, unchanging, and forever! '*Ram*' is that aspect of universal life that is permeating throughout, knowing throughout, omniscient and, therefore, worthy of our undivided attention in meditation! '*Madhu*' means sweet and pleasing and in this mantra takes on the higher meaning of blissful, blessed and forever free from any pain or discomfort. And finally, '*hum*' translates as we, that aspect of self that is common to all humanity as 'I', the royal we, that includes all life, all action, all thought and all time, space and beyond!

So, literally, *Amaram Hum, Madhuram Hum* translates as 'undying self am I, sweetest self am I' and in meditation this meaning is refined and simplified to: 'I am immortal, I am blissful.'

To get the correct pronunciation of *Amaram Hum, Madhuram Hum* practice saying: '*amar*' as 'a' (as spoken in 'far') + '*mar*' (as in '*mar*' your thoughts); '*ram*' as 'rum' (the drink); '*hum*' just like it sounds and '*madhu*' as '*mad*' (spoken as 'mud') + '*hu*' (spoken as 'who'). Put it all together and we get: *amar rum hum mudwho rum hum*…(listen to Infinite Peace audio recording (CD or MP3) to hear correct pronunciation).

Now all that's left to do is to gently take this magnificent mantra and practice repeating it. Sit comfortably, with eyes closed, in an easy, relaxed posture and just, very gently, like you're rocking a little baby in your arms, start to repeat this mantra quietly using your voice - *Amaram Hum, Madhuram Hum*. With each repetition of the sound also resonate the meaning 'I am Immortal, I am Blissful' on the canvas of your mind.

After a few minutes of peacefully repeating this mantra as a vocal vibration, gently shift the repetition of *Amaram Hum, Madhuram Hum* to the inside, so that no more gross sound is heard. The mantra's vibration is only happening inside your mind and inner senses, along with the unbroken and parallel repetition of its meaning: 'I am Immortal, I am Blissful.'

Keep repeating mantra in this way – very, very gently; very, very softly; with no rush or force from anywhere within your being – and just naturally allow its soothing, calming influence to fill you with peace, comfort and a sense of completeness and total ease!

In this way, successfully repeating mantra's sound and meaning together, your practice of mantra meditation will deepen and mature!

Transformation Meditation Is More Than You Think!

A common reaction from people when I mention meditation is: I have tried to meditate but I can't because I have too many thoughts in my mind. This reaction shows a general misconception about what meditation is. The purpose of the mind is to think. You wouldn't want to change the functioning of the eyes from seeing or the functioning of the ears from hearing, so why try to stop the mind from thinking? The types of thoughts or how many thoughts you have in your mind while you are meditating are not a problem. You don't need to try to control these thoughts. Controlling thoughts or controlling your mind is impossible, as thoughts just seem to appear from nowhere. If I say to you right now, "Don't think of white elephants," the first thought you have will be of white elephants. You see, you can't stop your thoughts from coming by telling yourself not to think them. You can, however, tune-in to the space of meditation if you place your attention between or behind the thoughts. If you think, "I am meditating," between "I" and "am" is space and between "am" and "meditating" is also space. You become aware that this space is like the canvas or background on which the thought appears. A painting is painted on a canvas. The canvas is always there behind the paint as the space is there behind the thought.

In yogic theory, from which Transformation Meditation was developed, the mind is considered to be a field of consciousness. Thoughts are called *vrittis* or waves of perception. They come into the mind as if from nowhere or from pure space or consciousness. Thought is nothing but a modification of the space itself that now appears as a thought or a wave of perception on the canvas of your mind. Science tells us that physical forms are not really solid. They are a group of molecules or atoms moving in space. Deepak Chopra (1993), the famous Ayurvedic physician and author, states that even our physical bodies are 99.9% space. Thoughts are also space or Pure Consciousness that appear as waves in the field of the mind. When ice is heated it melts into water and when water is heated it becomes steam, yet it is still H_2O. Just as the frozen water appears as ice and when heated becomes water and then steam, so thoughts move through the body (brain) or mind and, subsiding, return to their source or Pure Consciousness. Using this analogy, the physical body is to ice as thoughts are to water and consciousness is to steam. In essence they are the same substance.

This system of meditation is called Transformation Meditation because the individual waking state of consciousness is transformed into a higher state of awareness. The mental, or thinking, state is transformed back into its originality of pure space or consciousness. In the deep sleep state you are free from troubles, concerns, worries, agitation and even physical pains. When you wake up, as soon as you say, "I am awake," your mind and thoughts come in and the problems return.

There exists a higher state of consciousness where, even while awake, you can remain at ease and at peace. You can wake up from the waking state of consciousness into the state of higher consciousness. This state is dear to all of us; it's our true nature. You have been in this state any time you have felt easy, peaceful, in love or in harmony with nature. When you remember these moments, you realize this potential is there within you all the time.

Remember when you were in a good mood? Then things didn't seem to affect you in the same way. Troubling situations may have arisen but you didn't seem bothered by them. In this higher state of consciousness you are not suppressing your feelings. You still have a full range of emotions; however, you do not become devastated or react as severely to things that are not in your control. You still have thoughts and feelings; and, further, you are aware that you are more than your thoughts and feelings, and you are not limited by them. You are the Knower or observer of your thoughts.

While meditating, you tune into yourself as the Knower of the mind and thoughts. Changing the thoughts once they have arisen, or trying to think more positively, although useful for developing a more positive approach to life, is only part of this practice. It would be impossible to change the thousands of thoughts that come into your mind every day. However, you, as the watcher or Knower, can watch these thoughts or waves of perception. The waves of the ocean are nothing but the same ocean water; we call them waves, but they are still ocean water. You do not have to see your thoughts as anything separate from the ocean of your consciousness. They do not have power over You, the Knower, unless you choose to give them your attention or become mixed or identified with them and begin to treat them as real or important. With the practice of Transformation Meditation you develop a great power to transform the way your thinking mechanism works. You are no longer a victim of your mind and thought process. You become free from the problematic or stressful state and experience a higher state of consciousness. You can easily become aware of this higher state of consciousness because it is inherent in you, at the very source of all your thinking.

There are currently over two hundred and fifty psychotherapeutic theories and numerous self-help strategies and personal growth seminars. In order to find the secrets to successful living we must first examine the lives of people who have practiced a system that resulted in this success and who lived a balanced life. I have observed, through my study of Eastern philosophy, and, more specifically, yogic science and psychology, that an optimum, healthy psychological state has been obtained by its practitioners.

The yogic system of meditation was first recorded by the sage Patanjali in the fourteenth century B.C. The methods in this work of Patanjali have been shown to be effective through centuries of practice. The result of the practice of meditation is that one achieves a superior state of physical health and psychological well being. There have been numerous interpretations of these ancient teachings that describe this philosophy. Some of them can be confusing and are not easily adaptable to modern-day living. Out of that confusion many misconceptions have developed about meditation practice. Transformation Meditation is a scientific approach that clarifies these Eastern teachings and allows one to experience the benefits of meditation quickly and easily.

Why Do You Suffer?
The Essential Purpose of Human Life

There is an old story that portrays how the mind works to bring about suffering. Two young men decided to travel from India to America to gain financial success. After one year in America, one of the men established himself in a lucrative position, married and became financially successful. The other young man met with misfortune and became ill and died. The first young man met someone who was returning to India and asked him to please relay the message to both families regarding his success and his friend's misfortune. The messenger returned to India and relayed the messages. However, he mixed up the names, reporting to one set of parents that their son had died when, in fact, he had married and become financially successful. To the other family, he reported that their son had become rich and married when, in fact, he had met with great misfortune and had died. The parents of the son who died, but were told that he had become successful, celebrated and rejoiced with the news. The family of the son who actually became successful, but were told that he had died, began to mourn with intense grief.

This story portrays how the mind functions. It becomes identified with the thought of either death or happiness and wealth, believes it to be the truth, and either suffers or rejoices. How many times have you suffered needlessly after hearing the wrong information? Have you experienced a misfortune or difficult situation that turned out in the long run to be beneficial for you in some way? Maybe you learned from it or grew from the experience, or it was a warning sign that helped you to avoid a dangerous situation in the future. Your mind has been unskillfully trained through the development of concepts and belief systems to experience all situations according to past experiences. It is limited by these concepts and unable to see the whole picture or complete truth. A blind man touching only the trunk of an elephant would conclude that an elephant is long and thin.

Babies in the womb, with all their needs totally taken care of, are completely connected and at one with their mother. The result is that no fear of separation or sense of duality can arise for them. However, as soon as birth takes place and the umbilical cord is cut, separation is experienced. At that time, due to this new dualistic perspective, fear and pain begin. The infant, whose essence was Pure Consciousness, without thoughts, beliefs and concepts, was experiencing Oneness with everything. Then, at birth or some time soon after, they become a separate person. This is a necessary step in development. Children have to begin to view themselves as separate people, develop independence and learn to take care of themselves. So what goes wrong at this point? Children, in the process of developing their own ego or sense of individuality, forget the experience of Pure Consciousness or their essential nature of Oneness with everything. The idea, then, is not to change this necessary developmental process, but to be able to develop as a fully functioning, independent person and simultaneously experience one's essential nature. The quality of this Pure Consciousness state, or essential nature, is a sense of ease and peacefulness.

When you look at newborn babies, you never think they are bad or anything less then perfect expressions of life. Why, then, do people judge or criticize themselves or others? It is the faulty mechanism or ineffective training that has created the problem, not the innocent, perfect expression of life that was brought into this world some years before. We need to remember this and treat the faulty mechanism, not blame the person or ourselves.

Patanajli Yog Darshan (Shyam, 2001) states that all pain and suffering are due to ignorance of the Self. Modern psychology, a science still comparatively in its infancy, suggests that they are due to one's genetic makeup, childhood experiences, parental influences or learned behaviors and thinking processes. Patanjali takes us to the source of the problem. He answers the question: What is the mechanism in a human being that causes the destructive genetics patterns, harmful parenting and improper thinking? As we know, many people who were brought up in the most abusive environments have risen above their situations and gone on to excel in life. What is different about these individuals and those who continue their self-defeating patterns? We can't continue to blame our parents or their parents or even the proverbial Adam and Eve. We have to take responsibility and learn how the faulty mechanisms of the mind and nervous system work. As soon as you train the mechanism of the mind and strengthen the nervous system through the practice of meditation, you will experience what is called the fourth state of consciousness, or knowledge of the Self. The workings of this human system are then transformed.

The essential purpose of human life, according to the yogic system, is to become aware of, or to realize, one's own true nature. The term "to realize" is used because this is not something that one needs to find, discover or create. Instead, it is the very essence of who we all are. We, therefore, realize what already exists. It is only because one has shifted their attention away from the experience of their essential nature of Pure Consciousness towards the body, mind, and emotions that they are, then, not aware of this realized state. Most people experience life in an identified state of consciousness called the waking state. They forget that they exist as the Knower of the experience. When one is aware of oneself as the very life force, or Knower, one is not identifying as only the changing thoughts and feelings. One is in touch with the life itself and experiences the bliss of the very life or higher Self. This explains why one person on vacation, or out in a peaceful natural setting, remains troubled or agitated while another person in the same setting, or even in a busy city, remains peaceful. This shows that it is not the setting or experience, rather it is the condition of the mind that determines the quality of our experience.

Most people are striving for happiness, peace, contentment and freedom from pain and suffering. This state of true peace or happiness is our essential nature; it cannot be found outside of us. The existential questions, such as: Who am I? and What is my purpose? are all answered when one experiences one's true nature. This state is what Abraham Maslow (1970) calls a peak or transcendent experience. His findings show that everyone has had or can have a peak experience. This experience is not necessarily a consequence of any religious belief or particular denomination, as those from all groups have such experiences. This experience, according to Maslow (1970), can be scientifically tested. In fact, he states that in interviews, "non theistic" people said that they had more religious or transcendent experiences than conventionally religious people. This "peak experience" may initially last for only a few seconds or minutes; however, it is a state filled with knowledge and is also often referred to in yogic science as the "question-less" state. As soon as one brings the attention to the Knower of any experience this peak experience occurs, as one has transcended the mind. This can be accomplished even at the beginning stages of meditation.

One might ask, if everyone is striving for happiness, why is it that some people rob banks, kill other people, and commit acts that seem harmful to themselves and others? No matter what action a person is taking, they ultimately believe it will bring them happiness. Even when someone kills another human being, they do it because they believe, incorrectly of course, that they will feel better. Although these acts might bring moments of relief, they do not bring long term satisfaction. Instead, they create more pain and suffering.

What most people incorrectly believe will bring them happiness is the fulfillment of a desire. It is very tiring to manipulate, and impossible to have, everything the way you desire it all the time, the very nature of life being a state of constant change. When one desires something and then attains it, there is a sense of momentary happiness or fulfillment. As a result, a mistaken belief is developed that if all the desires are met, one will have a happy life. If you analyze your own life and that of others, you can become aware that this is a false belief. For no matter how many desires one fulfills, another one is waiting just around the corner. Yet, there exists for many people the false belief that more money, success, power, love, etc., will bring total happiness and satisfaction. Therefore, most people, in their striving for happiness, keep living out their desires. When a desire is met they are happy; when a desire is not met they suffer. Fulfilling our desires, although necessary for life, will never bring lasting happiness or peace. In fact, it is the very need to have the things one desires that prevents this. When you get what you want and feel momentarily happy, you then fear its loss because you believe that is what brought you happiness.

This can be seen with the addictive personality which desires the substance, feels good for a while after getting it and then suffers again, needing more when the effect is gone. This addictive behavior applies not only to substances but to people, things, power, money, love, work, etc. Every human being, however, is born with desires, and it is through these desires that one manifests one's life. If one does not seek happiness through fulfilling desires, how will one function in life and achieve happiness? If you follow a desire to its source, through the practice of meditation, you can become aware that behind or between the very thoughts that make up the desire is a state of Pure Consciousness or peace. The desire, then, is seen as a passing wave of perception, and one has the choice to act on it or not. As Swami Shyam (1985) expresses:

> The technique is simply to sit still, watch the space and acquaint yourself with your own Self, the pure Knower. Once you have attained this, you have gained the mastery of controlling desires, which means that any time you want to formulate a desire, just do it, and when you want to dismantle it, just do that. If you want to execute a desire, then release the ability from within yourself and fulfill that desire. If you want to experience pain or bondage, then you are free to create that also. But since you have mastery or you are the master, then everything is just your own form and you are forever the blissful Lord, the Master.

When the mind no longer identifies itself with the problematic waking state of consciousness and experiences Pure Consciousness, one becomes the master rather than the victim of one's own mental and emotional functioning. Regardless of one's dysfunctional childhood or life experience, one can transform the workings of the mind and learn to disengage from mistaken beliefs, desires and concepts that lead to pain and suffering. Instead, one can enjoy the inner state of peace and live in this state of higher consciousness. The proof is there as this state has been obtained and lived by many Self-realized beings throughout history. From their example and by having your own experience of this state through the practice of meditation, you can become aware that you, too, can achieve this state of higher consciousness.

MEDITATE NOW!
TWELVE SECRETS TO
DOUBT FREE MEDITATION

Would you like to feel peaceful, relaxed, easy, joyful, blissful, clear, balanced, healthy, fearless and in tune with your true nature?

But you find it hard to sit with your eyes closed to meditate?

1. **Your mind will not feel easy sitting to meditate**

   When you first start, you must give up the idea that you should feel easy and relaxed when you start to meditate.

   This is the main reason why people have a difficult time meditating. They get frustrated as the mind is filled with so many thoughts such as: "This is to be done, and why is this not happening like I think it should?" To begin to meditate you must expect that your mind will keep thinking. Just as the human body wakes up every morning – that's its nature - in the same way, the mind generates thoughts without your control or demand.

2. **Accept whatever you are thinking**

   You can't always choose your thoughts and often you don't even want to entertain them, but they come anyway, of their own accord! No one wants to be afraid, anxious, angry, annoyed and think negative thoughts about themselves or others, yet, sometimes, it happens. The eyes see, the ears hear and we never expect them to do otherwise, so why expect your mind not to think thoughts?

3. Close your eyes and watch the space

As soon as you close your eyes, what do you see? What appears in front of your closed eyes may be a vast space of darkness with some light or color in it - like a canvas where all the thoughts, images and impressions are projected in front of you. Yet, the actual canvas of your awareness, upon which all these thoughts are projecting on to, remains forever, the same pure space, unchanged by this passing parade of changing impressions, infinite images and fantastic light shows.

4. Watch with inner vision

As soon as you close your eyes, meditation is right there, omnipresent as that space that appears right in front of your closed eyes. It's as if you are now see-ing with an inner eye, sometimes called the third eye. That is the inner vision - which sees the vastness of pure space, free from any impressions formed on it - just like the water in the oceans is always water, even when it appears as foam, waves, or spray.

5. Repeat mantra … watch the breath

As thoughts appear in the mind and take your attention away from the pure space, one can use a mantra or watch one's breath to bring your attention back to the source of your thought - You. Just repeat the mantra silently to yourself, over and over again, or watch the flow of your breath, gently in-and-out.

6. Thoughts will come and go

You will notice that your thoughts come and go - just like waves rising and falling in the ocean. They are never a problem for you. You recognize them as only passing waves of perception – temporary, changing and impermanent.

7. Back to mantra

When you get involved in thoughts and start to get carried away from medi-tation, you have the power to go back to repeating the mantra whenever you choose to.

8. Never mind when you forget

If you forget to return to mantra and remain involved in your thinking, then, no problem, you'll go back to mantra whenever you remember. Sometimes some organization and reflection of your thought happens first, before the freedom to let the thought go unfolds.

9. Watch the Space

Remember, whether you are engaged in thought or not, the space existing before, during and after all thought, remains forever shining just like the sun. Sometimes it gets clouded over with thoughts, and even then, it still remains shining! You can follow a thought to its source and observe, from that vantage point, the space from where thought came and to where it returns.

10. Who is watching? The Knower

You, as the one always watching, becomes your focus in meditation. The very Knower of all the thoughts, impressions, visions, scenes, senses, body, mind, and emotions is always there. That Knower you always are.

Knower permeates your mind as knowing, knowledge and the one who always knows, yet Knower remains forever free as pure, unchanging and perfectly complete – You!

11. Always a perfect meditation

Just taking the time to sit and watch is a perfect meditation. Even if your meditation is filled with thinking, rehashing the day or planning for the next, the one time you bring your attention to Knower you gain tremendous power to meditate and receive all its many benefits. Any efforts that you make to sit and watch and know are always beneficial.

Always remember - the meditative state happens by itself, just like you fall asleep, begin to dream and then wake up. You exist throughout as Knower!

12. Do it regularly

Regularity in your meditation practice is essential. Like anything else that you become proficient at, repetition is the secret. The more you practice, the more you benefit!

Yet, unlike training for a sports competition or a musical performance (long, arduous hours of practice for a brief event), through meditation you actually experience that state of peace and perfection in every practice!

Therefore, although it does takes regular repetition, you should always practice with the awareness that Knower is forever unaffected by any mental impressions.

Through meditation you will come to know your true nature - pure, free and forever!

Sixteen Effects of Meditation

1. You feel relaxed.

2. You feel peaceful.

3. You feel joyful with a joy that is not the thrill of victory. It's a blissful state unlike the joy of attaining any desired object.

4. You begin to see meditation as your greatest birthright. In your daily life all your activity is organized and focused to allow enough time for meditation.

5. Your intuitive awareness becomes so clear that the instant you see a person you know them. There will never be any misunderstanding, just as a mirror never finds difficulty in knowing any object reflected on it.

6. You will feel a great balance in yourself and never be bound by anything or anyone.

7. You will have more love, compassion and concern for everyone and become so generous that you will not think in terms of gain and loss when the call comes to serve a person who is, in any way, needy. Rather, you will know it as a concrete fact that that person is none other then your very own Self.

8. You will feel that your states of body and mind are vastly improving.

9. You will develop your power of detachment. All things, which had a binding influence on you, will lose their power over you as your strength unfolds, making you ready to face anything.

10. You will feel that your heart and mind are always expanding and that you are realizing the truth of the world, of the soul, and of God and that these are not separate from the truth of your very own Self.

11. You will feel that you are growing towards the infinite. Things of a finite nature will not create any anxiety, care or fear in you, even when they change.

12. In you only such desires will arise, the execution of which will result in service to others and peace to yourself.

13. You will be more decisive, energetic, fearless and dynamic! When a thought arises you will know what needs to be done.

14. You will feel a direct relationship to the almighty creator as a unique manifestation of creative intelligence, and begin to love your own creation.

15. For you, life in stability and life in change will be one and the same.

16. You will love and live for the purpose of making everyone higher in awareness. You'll flow in accordance with the Universal Will, which is creating, maintaining, dissolving, and recreating, again and again, with its own eternal law!

(adapted from an unpublished writing by Swami Shyam)

THE FOUR STATES OF CONSCIOUSNESS

Waking

Each morning you wake up and begin to think. Your daily desires arise and, subsequently, translate into their related actions. This is known as the waking state of consciousness. It is your total experience of the world, forms, people, interactions and experiences.

In this state there is some happiness and some joy, some of this and some of that, totally based on your daily continuum of related experiences, which are always changing. If life is going well, you are happy. If you get what you want, you are happy. If you don't get what you want and begin to experience pain, disease or uneasiness you may start to feel unhappy, sad or depressed.

Dream

Every night, when you go to sleep, you dream. These are mental images, pictures, events or movies created by your mind. There is even a sense that you are not confined to your physical body for, in a dream, you can go anywhere and experience anything!

Deep Sleep

Every night when you fall asleep this state comes automatically. In deep sleep there exists no mind, thoughts or impressions. Patanjali, the father of Yog, defined this state of consciousness as a sustained thought of nothingness.

No matter how many worries you had in the waking state, no matter how much pain you were in or how much you were suffering, you remain at peace as long as you are in deep sleep. Every night, in deep sleep, you are blissful. And then, since deep sleep is changing and transitory, you wake up!

Meditative or Fourth State - *Turiya Awasthaa*

When you practice meditation you automatically transcend the waking, dream and deep sleep states and begin to know this fourth state. Since it is permanent, forever and never changing, it is our natural, essential state of existence.

This fourth state becomes covered by the other three states much like the sun gets covered by clouds. It's always there, even when the other three states take place, just like the sun remains always shining behind the clouds. The meditative or fourth state is always at the back of all your thoughts, images and impressions just like the artist's canvas sits, unnoticed, behind the painting, providing the backdrop and foundation upon which the artist creates his vision.

In this fourth state the bliss of pure awareness is forever shining like the sun. And, with practice, this pure awareness can be fully realized as your own true nature – pure, free and forever. Through meditation practice you wake up from the waking state into the fourth state – *Turiya Awasthaa*.

Just like in deep sleep, which is experienced nightly, in this fourth state you are free from all troubles, pain and agitation. But, unlike deep sleep, in *Turiya Awasthaa* you can function in the world as an aware, sentient being. You are living the free state of pure consciousness.

In this meditative state, the human being (consisting of body, mind, ego and senses) is seen as the instrumentality through which You, the pure Self being, experiences the world, its forms and their interactions. However, the knowledge is there that you are not limited just to this human instrumentality. You remain the unlimited Knower of this limited human being and, therefore, are not affected by the changing, impermanent nature of the body, mind and senses.

You reside in your true nature, the fourth state:
Pure, free and forever!

How Stress Can Affect You

In a stressful situation the body initiates 'Fight-or-Flight':

1. The sympathetic nervous system stimulates receptors in the heart that make it beat faster and harder, preparing you to fight or run away. This can cause the coronary arteries to constrict.

2. The brain causes other organs such as the adrenal glands to secrete stress hormones such as adrenaline, and steroids such as cortisol, which circulate in the blood until they reach the heart.

A series of physiological reactions occurs:

1. The muscles contract, helping to fortify the body's armor to help protect it from injury.

2. The metabolism speeds up the heart rate and the amount of blood pumped with each beat increases.

3. Breathing increases, providing more oxygen, to do battle or run from danger.

4. The digestive system shuts down, diverting energy to the muscles that are needed in order to fight or run.

5. Arteries in our arms and legs constrict so that less blood will be lost if you become wounded.

6. Blood clots more quickly to slow blood loss due to injury.

Chronic stress can cause:

1. Tension, anxiety and/or depression.

2. More blood clots in the arteries reducing blood flow to the heart.

3. Arteries in the heart to constrict which can cause spasms. When a coronary artery goes into spasm it can injure the lining of the artery leading to cholesterol deposits and plaque build-up.

4. High blood pressure.

5. Weakened nervous and immune system.

(Adapted from Dr. Dean Ornish's Program for Reversing Heart Disease. Random House, 1990.)

Breathing Techniques
(Praanaayaam)

If someone were to ask you if you know how to breathe you probably would laugh. We all know that breathing is necessary for life; however, the way you breathe has an effect on your overall health and state of well-being. *Praanaayaam*, or breath control, is an ancient yogic system that increases energy and creates balance and overall health. Certain techniques were developed to regulate one's energies by training the breathing mechanism. The breath is the part of the autonomic nervous system that is both automatic and voluntarily controlled. You can't control your heart rate or blood pressure at will; however, you can easily control your breath. The breath is very closely linked with the emotions. When one is calm, the breath is deep and slow. When one is tense, angry or fearful, the breath is held or becomes irregular, short or difficult. Therefore, by controlling the breath one can regulate the emotions and create a sense of calmness. These techniques have also been known to strengthen the nervous system and to switch on the parasympathetic part of the autonomic nervous system. This can be very helpful for those restless nights when you are trying to fall asleep and your mind keeps racing with all kinds of thoughts. By changing one's orientation from a sympathetic or more active mode to a parasympathetic mode, one's nervous system can rest, relax and repair.

The technique of diaphragmatic breathing helps to move the diaphragm so that it presses on the lower portion of the lungs and releases all the carbon dioxide as one exhales. There is then room to expand the abdomen on the inhalation and to take in a larger supply of fresh oxygen. This oxygen and "*praan*," or life force energy, that is taken in with the breath then oxygenates and revitalizes all the cells, organs, glands and the brain. When one is anxious the lungs fill with carbon dioxide and the introduction of fresh oxygen is difficult. This often occurs during an anxiety or panic attack. The lungs fill up with carbon dioxide and cannot take in oxygen. You feel as if you cannot breathe. Diaphragmatic breathing then helps you to exhale all the carbon dioxide and makes room to bring in more oxygen. The fresh oxygen creates a calming effect and strengthens the nervous and immune systems. This type of breathing also reverses the stress response by providing more oxygenation of the blood. This results in greater mental acuity and improved general health.

Another technique, called alternate nostril breathing, involves alternately inhaling through one nostril and then exhaling through the other. If you check throughout the day you will notice, unless your nose is stuffed due to a cold or allergy, that one nostril is usually more open than the other. This seems to switch every few hours over the course of the day. In right-handed people, when the right nostril is clogged and the left is more open, then the right side of the brain or the creative side is dominant. Conversely, when the left side is clogged and the right nostril is more open, the left side of the brain, or the analytic side, is more active. If you are having trouble with creativity or being analytical or even sleeping at night, it's interesting to check which nostril is more open. By using the alternate nostril technique, you can balance the right and left sides of the brain, soothe and purify the nervous system, and cleanse and open the nasal passages. This normalizes the metabolic process and combats the detrimental effects of stress.

Longevity can be measured by the number of breaths one takes per minute. Dogs and cats have a faster breathing rate then humans, so their life span is shorter. Those species that breathe at a slower rate per minute live longer. They do not need to take in as much oxygen to sustain the body. The lungs and heart do not have to labor as hard and vital energy is conserved. If you want to live a longer and healthier life, then daily take up this practice of *praanaayaam*; your great-grandchildren will be glad you did.

PRACTICING BREATHING TECHNIQUES

Deep Abdominal Breathing

1. Exhale all the breath while gently pulling in the abdomen.

2. Begin inhaling while puffing out the abdomen.

3. Gently bring the breath upwards, allowing the rib cage to move to the side; then continue bringing the breath up, thus expanding the chest.

4. Slowly begin to exhale the breath reversing this process, exhaling from the chest, allowing the rib cage and then the abdomen to gently go down.

Benefits:

Deep abdominal breathing reverses the stress reaction by providing more oxygenation of the blood resulting in greater relaxation, better emotional balance and control, greater mental clarity and acuity, and greatly improved general health. It switches on the parasympathetic part of the involuntary nervous system, which allows the system to rest, relax and repair. Your lung capacity will gradually increase so you will become less winded by exertion.

Alternate-Nostril Breathing

1. Making a gentle fist with the right hand, extend the thumb and the last two fingers, leaving a space for the nose.

2. With the thumb, close off the right nostril and exhale through the left.

3. Using the deep abdominal breathing, inhale through the left nostril then close it off with the last two fingers and exhale through the right nostril. Continue by inhaling through the right nostril, closing it off and exhaling through the left.

Benefits:

Alternate-nostril breathing can help soothe, purify and strengthen the nervous system. It can help you to develop control of your body, mind and emotions. It also helps to increase mental alertness, cleanse and open the nasal passages, normalize the metabolic process and combat the overall detrimental effects of stress.

THIS IS MEDITATION

Eight Steps to Meditation Practice

1. Sit with your back comfortably straight, your head and neck aligned with the spine as much as possible.

2. Gently close your eyes.

3. Notice the space that you see in front of your closed eyes.

4. Make an imaginary circle in the middle of the space, the circumference of which is according to your own imagination.

5. From the center of the circle, coming as if to your eyes, begin to silently repeat the mantra, *Amaram Hum Madhuram Hum,* while remembering its meaning, I am Immortal I am blissful.

6. Focus your attention on the last syllable of each word spoken in order to continue focusing the attention on the first syllable of the next word. Continue this repetition with one-pointedness.

7. Be aware of the Knower who knows how to speak the mantra, listen to the words in silence, and know the meaning contained in these words.

8. During this period, thoughts will come, arise, stay or go away. You remain neutral to them and non-dealing with them. Your attention goes to focus on the Knower, realizing that the Knower is Pure Consciousness, Pure Existence and Pure Bliss. Continue meditating and holding this realization for a few minutes, considering that this Self or I or Knower is the source; everything, everywhere.

Benefits:

Reverses the 'fight-or-flight' (stress) reaction; helps lower blood pressure and cho-lesterol levels; reduces the heart rate and the oxygen requirement of the body by 10-20% in the first 3 minutes (this is also an effect produced by drug medications prescribed to lower high blood pressure, yet meditation is 100% natural and life-supporting and, therefore, has no detrimental side-effects); increases awareness and alertness; unfolds a state of Oneness and allows you to experience unity with your self and your world.

How to Transform Tension and Stress into Relaxation and Ease

1. When you are experiencing a situation in which you feel tension and unpleasant emotions, ask yourself the question, in what way would I like this situation to be different?

2. When you notice you are feeling tense, then watch the tension as it is approaching from the distance. Once it has come, accept it. Do not try to push it away or suppress it, or get angry at yourself for reacting, because that will make you more tense. Just recognize and observe what you are feeling and allow yourself to experience the symptoms in your body.

3. Now, begin to breathe using the abdominal breathing technique, slowly and deeply. As you change your breathing pattern, notice that you can begin to relax and change your thinking pattern. The breath is very closely connected to your mind and emotions. Check your body and see if there is any tension in your back, neck or shoulders; if so, take a deep breath and consciously give yourself the message to relax that area of your body.

4. Notice if you want to fight, argue or run from the situation and then follow the next steps to begin to change your thinking about the situation.

5. Recognize what you are telling yourself that you want from the situation. If there is anything that you can practically do to change the situation then decide to do it; if not, then you must accept what is actually happening rather then trying to fight it, mentally and emotionally. Give yourself the message that, as there is nothing you can do to change it, there is no point in having your mind dwell on it.

6. To stop dwelling on useless thoughts, you can elicit the relaxation response by placing you attention on the breath and slowing down the number of breaths you take per minute. Then start repeating the mantra, allowing the thoughts to come and go; then place your attention on the observer of the thoughts and gently bring the attention back to the breath or mantra whenever it gets involved in the thoughts.

Chart:
Non-Meditator's Mind/
Meditator's Mind

This chart explains the meditative process called de-identification. The upper part to the chart shows how the mind functions in someone who does not meditate or use any similar type of method. The lower part shows the mind of someone who practices meditation.

Non-Meditator's Mind

The first circle shows that we are all the same Self or pure consciousness. When the Self or pure being, using the mind, mixes with the thoughts (waves of perception) this identification process takes place and it is called waking state of consciousness or ignorance of the true Self. In this state you experience mental and emotional suffering or happiness—but this type of happiness will always have its opposite, unhappiness.

Meditator's Mind

The first circle shows that we are all the same Self or pure consciousness. While meditating you undo the mixture of the Self and mind. You become aware of the Observer or Knower of the mind and thought. Then you have the ability to de-identify with the waves of the mind as your attention is now placed on the one who is knowing the mind, the very YOU, Knower. This evokes the fourth state of consciousness or Knowledge of the Self. In this state you are aware of your true nature—peace, freedom and bliss.

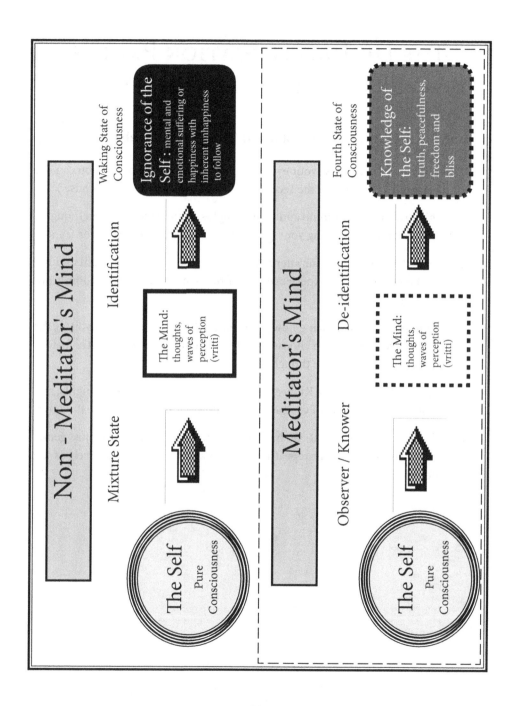

THE DE-IDENTIFICATION PROCESS
HOW TO STOP WORRYING AND ENJOY YOUR LIFE

Six Steps to Freedom from Disturbing Thoughts and Feelings

1. Sit in a quiet place, close your eyes and begin to relax your body. (You can use a breathing technique or the second part of the deep relaxation exercise.)

2. Begin to observe your mind and your thoughts, noticing how certain thoughts keep repeating or carrying your attention into a pattern of worries or fears.

3. Notice that if you put your attention on the pause after one thought and before the next one, you experience a brief moment of peace or freedom from the effect of the thought.

4. Repeat the mantra, noticing how other thoughts come and go and you, as the master of your mind, can choose to put your attention on the mantra instead of paying attention to the thoughts.

5. Be aware that you are the Knower or observer of your mind and thoughts, and begin to become aware of yourself as the Knower unmixed with the thoughts.

6. Whenever you notice that you have become mixed with a thought, just gently remind yourself to again repeat the mantra and be aware of yourself as the Knower.

Various Meditation Techniques

There are many variations of the techniques of meditation that you may use. The following is a list of a few of them. Remember while practicing any meditation technique that thoughts are not a problem to you, the meditator. You can just watch them and know they are waves of perception that arise, stay and then pass. The Pure Consciousness is always present and each wave is just a modification of that, just as a wave in the ocean is the same ocean water. (Also listen to the audio recording, Infinite Peace, for guided meditations using some of these variations.)

1. Repeat mantra silently to yourself

This basic mantra meditation technique should be practiced always with the awareness that you, the Knower, are repeating the mantra and then bringing your attention to the very Knower that is you.

2. Repeat mantra and watch the pause:

Notice the quiet space between each repetition of the mantra, knowing that bliss is forever present in the pause and also at the back of all the thoughts.

3. Repeat mantra while counting

You can either use a set of beads called maala beads and on each repetition move to the next bead (similar to a rosary), or you can count after each repetition until reaching 108. This number is considered a powerful number in yogic philosophy.

4. Repeat the mantra out loud

This technique is referred to as chanting and can assist you in becoming relaxed and focused. It can also enhance the silent meditation which can follow the chanting.

5. Create you own technique

As long as the basic elements are there you can use any object of focus, such as your breath, a candle, or a flower. At some point you can close your eyes and watch. As long as you close your eyes and are in touch with the observer or Knower, the meditation will unfold perfectly, almost by itself. You can just watch the space at the back of your closed eyes.

Sometimes the mantra will come easily and smoothly. You don't have to repeat it in the same rhythm as your breath, though it might coordinate on its own. After some time, you may get tired of repeating it. Then you can shorten the words or just continue by watching the space that has unfolded. The mantra is a tool to get you to know the space. Once you are there, experiencing a state of peace or bliss, just enjoy! (Also see "This is Meditation," in this manual.)

Progressive Deep Relaxation

(To be read out slowly and softly to you by a family member or close friend)

Relax on your back, arms at your side, palms turned up toward the ceiling, for deep relaxation. You will be alternately contracting and then relaxing each part of the body.

Bring the awareness to the right foot and leg - stretch out the leg, squeeze it tightly, raise it up one foot off the floor - RELEASE. (Repeat for the left leg.) Roll the ankles from side-to-side and relax the legs.

Bring the awareness to the right arm - stretch out the arm, the fingers, making a fist, raise it one foot off the ground - squeeze tight - RELEASE. (Repeat for left arm.) Roll the wrists and relax them...

Squeeze in the buttocks, pulling in the anus muscles - tight! - RELEASE.

Inhale, puffing out the lower abdomen. On the signal we will let the breath gush out of an open mouth. Open - RELEASE. Inhale, allow the air to come up into the chest - open the mouth - RELEASE.

Keeping the arms in place on the floor, curl the shoulders up in front of you, almost bringing them together under the chin - RELEASE. Gently roll the head and neck once or twice, returning it to the balance point of the body.

Stretch out the face, open your mouth, stick out the tongue - RELEASE. Curl the face into a ball, squeeze in the lips, eyes, forehead - RELEASE.

Now that we have physically gone over the body, keeping it still, we'll have a mental check. With the mind we will go over each part of the body. If you encounter any tension, concentrate on releasing that tightness.

Bring the awareness into the toes, soles of the feet, tops of the feet, ankles, up the shins, calves (concentrating on releasing any tightness), back of the knees, knee caps, front of the thighs, back of the thighs. Bring the awareness into the fingertips, palms of the hands, back of the hands, wrists, forearms, elbows, upper arms.

Bring your awareness into the lower abdomen (pelvic region), upper abdomen (rib cage), relax all internal organs.

Be aware of the buttocks (concentrating on releasing any tension), base of the spine, now coming up the spinal column vertebra by vertebra, releasing the entire back as your awareness comes up, lower, middle back, upper. Release the shoulders from the neck outward, back of the neck, head, top of the head. Bring the awareness to the throat and lips, nose, cheeks, eyes, eyelids, eyebrows, forehead.

Bring the awareness to the breath. Without controlling the breath, witness the inhalations, exhalations. Standing apart, witnessing the flow of the breath. *(wait 1 minute before proceeding)*

Bring the awareness to the mind, witness the thoughts coming into the mind, remaining a few minutes, then drifting off without your attention being carried off on a thought. Stand apart, witnessing the flow of the mind. *(wait 1 minute before proceeding)*

Allow the body - breath- and mind to drift off - witness the peace and tranquility - consciously witnessing the peace within. *(wait 3 to 5 minutes before proceeding)*

Now begin to wiggle your fingers and toes, slowly awakening the body. *(pause)* Begin to stretch your arms over your head and slowly stretch the entire body - legs downward along the floor and arms above your head along the floor. *(pause)* Release and slowly roll onto your side into the fetal position. Rest in that position for a few moments. *(pause)* Slowly raise yourself up into a sitting position facing this way.

Now take in a few deep abdominal breaths. *(pause)* Now a few rounds of alternate nostril breathing. Now, bringing the breath back to normal, sit in silent meditation for a few minutes. As you are very relaxed after the deep relaxation, meditation will happen almost automatically by just closing your eyes and beginning a technique.

Four Stages of Mantra Meditation

The repetition of a mantra such as *Amaram Hum Madhuram Hum* is a useful technique in meditation. It is a tool that will help you to experience your own true nature. Learning new things, such as playing a musical instrument or speaking a foreign language, is often achieved through repetition. Mantra, although practiced with repetition, is not repeated with unawareness or mundane rote. It is meant as a practice which brings about power *(siddhi)* to reach the supreme state of consciousness. In this state there is silence within the mind, which becomes still *(shaant)* and eventually you will merge the mind, or individual awareness, with the whole, which is Pure Consciousness and Knowingness.

Every time you practice you obtain the result, as this fourth state of consciousness is always with you. Therefore, the practice should be done with the awareness that you are obtaining the result rather than you will obtain it someday in the distant future. The following is a focus for your repetition of mantra. You can experience these stages as you progress in your meditation. Mantra should be practiced with the focus that you, the Pure Consciousness, are meditating on Pure Consciousness.

1. The sound is heard by your ears *(baikhari vaani)*

In this stage you can repeat or sing the mantra out loud and then hear it silently inside your head.

2. The sound is spoken inside your mind *(madhyamaa vaani)*

Then you can repeat mantra silently so that it becomes more apparent that it is permeating your mind.

3. **The life pulsation is felt and the mantra is spread in the whole sky or universe** *(pashyanti vaani)*

   After many repetitions, one may become aware that there is no longer anybody there to perceive, as the individual awareness gets absorbed in the absolute space.

4. **All is Pure Existence and Consciousness** *(paraa vaani)*

   There is no time and space, there is nothing to describe about your experience.

Through mantra our mental being becomes subtler and subtler and vaster and vaster until perfect stillness or Oneness arises.

Recommended Reading List

Benson, H. (1975). *The Relaxation Response*. New York: Avon.

Benson, H. (1996). *Timeless Healing, The Power and Biology of Belief*. New York: Fireside.

Benson, H. & Stuart, E.M. (1993). *The Wellness Book: A Comprehensive Guide to Maintaining Health and Treating Stress Related Illness*. New York: Fireside.

Borysenko, J. (1987). *Minding The Body, Mending The Mind*. New York: Bantam.

Chopra, D. (1991). *Unconditional Life*. New York: Bantom.

Davis, M., Eshelman, E., McKay, M. (1982). *The Relaxation & Stress Reduction Workbook*. Oakland, CA: New Harbinger Publications.

Eaton, R. W. (2005). *Patanjali Yog Darshan: Wisdom of Meditation*. Boca Raton, FL: Transformation Meditation.com.

Kabat-Zinn, J. (1994). *Wherever You Go There You Are: Mindfulness Meditation in Everyday Life*. New York: Hyperion.

Kripalu staff (1981). *The Self-Health Guide*. Summit Station, PA: Kripalu Publications.

Ornish, D. (1990). *Dr. Dean Ornish's Program For Reversing Heart Disease*. New York: Random House.

Shyam, S. (1986). *Bhagavad Gita*. Delhi, India: Be All Publications.*

Shyam, S (2001). *Patanjali Yog Darshan*. Delhi, India: Be All Publications.*

Shyam, S. (1994). *Vision of Oneness. India*: International Meditation Institute.*

Siegel, Bernie (1986). Love, Medicine & Miracles. New York: Harper & Row.

* Books by Swami Shyam can be ordered from www.shyamswisdom.com

FOUNDATION SERIES QUIZ

If you have registered for the course and receive 70% correct or more on this quiz, you will receive a Certificate of Achievement by email within 14 days. To take this quiz and complete your course evaluation online, for your records, first mark your answers below. Then proceed to the link given in your registration confirmation email. Please email us if you require further assistance. quiz@transformationmeditation.com

1. What is the biggest misconception about meditation?

a. it is easy	b. you should not have any thoughts
c. you will fall asleep	d. you will become happy

2. Waves are to the ocean as thoughts are to:

a. Pure Consciousness	b. dreams
c. mind	d. waking state

3. What is the essential purpose of human life according to the yogic system?

a. to study	b. to realize one's true nature
c. to find the perfect vocation	d. to make money

4. What are the four states of consciousness?

a. dream, awake, daydream, sleep	b. conscious, unconscious, dream, meditative state
c. waking, dreaming, deep sleep, meditative state	d. waking, unconscious, sleep, beta

5. The 'fight-or-flight' response refers to:

a. a desire to be out of control	b. feeling like you want to fight or run away in a stressful situation
c. secretion of adrenaline and epinephrin; also increased blood pressure and heart rate.	d. both b and c

6. Mantra means:

a. man and trees	b. song
c. mind release	d. both a and b

7. The Knower is:

a. the mind	b. the true self
c. the body	d. the objects

8. Diaphragmatic breathing:

a. is done automatically by everyone	b. expands the abdomen in order for one to take in more oxygen
b. reverses the stress response	d. both b and c

9. De-identification means:

a. undoing the mixture of the mind and the Self	b. letting go of disturbing thoughts and feelings
c. putting your attention on the Knower	d. all the above: a, b and c

10. The four stages of mantra meditation are:

a. sound is heard in ears, sound is spoken inside the mind, life pulsation is felt, no time and space exist to describe the experience	b. singing, saying, hearing and internalizing
c. outside, inside, concentration, thougtlessness	d. awareness, consciousness, helpfulness and knowledge

COURSE EVALUATION FORM

Name: _____ Date: _____

Please rate the program according to the following criteria:
(5= excellent 4= good 3= satisfactory 2= needs improvement 1= poor)

	5	4	3	2	1
1. Quality of writing	☐	☐	☐	☐	☐
2. Ease of use	☐	☐	☐	☐	☐
3. Value of information	☐	☐	☐	☐	☐
4. Relevance to practice	☐	☐	☐	☐	☐
5. Quality of manuals and recordings	☐	☐	☐	☐	☐
6. Price of program	☐	☐	☐	☐	☐
7. Punctuality of delivery	☐	☐	☐	☐	☐
8. Overall quality of program	☐	☐	☐	☐	☐

9. What are the primary reasons for your enrolling in this practice?

   Interest in the subject _____ Personal growth _____

   Earning credits_____ Teaching _____ Other _____

10. Would you like additional courses on similar topics? _____

   If yes, check which ones: Breathing techniques _____

   Patanjali Yog Darshan _____ Bhagavad Gita _____

   Other methods of meditation _____Advanced training _____

11. Additional Comments:_____

   _____

   _____

Instructions: To take this Quiz and complete the Course Evaluation Form online, use the link provided in your registration confirmation email or email us for the link at quiz@transformationmeditation.com

OTHER COURSES FROM
TRANSFORMATIONMEDITATION.COM

Meditation Teacher Training, by Shree, Sherrie Wade

http://www.transformationmeditation.com/about_tt.htm

Doubt Free Meditation Foundation Series, by Shree, Sherrie Wade

http://www.transformationmeditation.com/about_fc.htm

Essence of Patanjali Yoga Sutras, by Brijendra, Robert William Eaton

http://www.transformationmeditation.com/about_es.htm

Essence of the Bhagavad Gita, by Glen Kezwer, Ph.D.

http://www.transformationmeditation.com/about_bg.htm

In the Stillness of Breath: Praanaayaam for Meditators, by Brijendra, Robert William Eaton

http://www.transformationmeditation.com/about-praanaayaam-course.htm

Made in the USA
Monee, IL
30 January 2024

52656602R00033